A Game of Thrones Feast of Characters:

The Juice Beneath the Game of Thrones Series on HBO

An Official Game of Thrones Character Guide

Table of Contents

INTRODUCTION

Game of Thrones is an epic fantasy show that has been airing on HBO since 2011. It concluded its sprawling fourth season on June 15, 2014. It has become increasingly popular over the last four years, inspiring a legion of passionate fans, and becoming HBO's most-viewed series, surpassing *The Sopranos*. It's also the most pirated show of all time, having a loyal viewership worldwide where people can't afford a HBO subscription. Needless to say, Game of Thrones has become the latest global cultural phenomenon, stimulating everything from angry discussions on internet message boards, to scholarly papers finding parallels between the politics of the show and the real world.

The show is based on George R.R. Martin's *A Song of Ice and Fire* series. Show-runners David Benioff and Dan Weiss pitched it to HBO as "Sopranos meets Middle-Earth", which is as accurate a one-line summary as this show will ever get. It mostly takes place in the fictional continent of Westeros, which is comprised of seven culturally and geographically distinct kingdoms. The seven kingdoms of Westeros – The North, The Isles and Rivers, The Vale, The Rock, The Reach, The Stormlands, and Dorne – are ruled by one king, who resides in King's Landing. The king sits atop an Iron Throne, a brutal, appropriately theatrical seat for the One True King, supposedly made from a thousand swords.

Westeros is based on medieval European culture, with a feudal, stratified society, far removed from our modern post-enlightenment values. Each of the seven kingdoms has a warden, belonging to a noble house. Much of the show is about the political intrigue and power struggles between various noble houses pursuing clashing interests, motivated by different reasons. Some are seeking justice, while others just want power for the sake of it.

Martin draws generously from history for inspiration, incorporating details from everything, be it the chaotic War of the Roses, or the ruthless Mongolian hordes. For the most part, the show feels like a grounded historical fiction, that is, until the dragons enter. Yes, there be dragons. And ice zombies, giants, magic baby smoke monsters, flaming swords, and much, much more.

Like the *Lord of The Rings* series, *Game of Thrones* uses its fantasy elements sparingly, and it pays great dividends. The fantasy in the show never overwhelms the drama, never makes for easy deux ex machinas. At its heart, the show is always a meditation on power, family, love, and revenge. If that doesn't do it for you, then there's also a lot of nudity, because this is an HBO show, and thus would be incomplete without copious shots of female breasts.

So let's dive into the various epic characters of this epic show, but be warned: Spoilers Are Coming.

1. Eddard Stark

Eddard "Ned" Stark, played by Sean Bean, is the quintessential good guy. He's the warden of the North, and lives in the snowy Winterfell, the capital of the North. The sigil of House Stark is a direwolf, and their motto is "Winter is Coming". The Starks ruled over the North for thousands of years, until Aegon the Conqueror invaded Westeros with his massive dragons almost three hundred years ago and made them wardens. Before the invasion, the seven kingdoms of Westeros were independent.

Ned Stark is as good a guy as you're going to get in Westeros. He's loyal, honorable, and lawful, almost to a fault. He has a strong sense of justice, and deeply believes in the laws of the kingdom. In the first episode, we see him behead a guy for breaking a sacred vow.

Ned is a close friend to King Robert Baratheon, who fought alongside him fifteen years ago in the Rebellion against the Targaryen dynasty. The seven kingdoms were conquered by Aegon Targaryen, and Targaryens ruled over Westeros for hundreds of years, until Robert Baratheon started a rebellion and usurped the last Targaryen king, Aerys II Targaryen, aka the Mad King.

Robert comes to Winterfell to ask Ned to become the new Hand of the King, chief advisor and executor of the King's orders, after the previous Hand of the King dies under suspicious circumstances. Despite the reservations of his wife, Catelyn Stark, the honorable Ned obeys the King and follows him to King's Landing, and assumes his new duties without wasting any time.

Ned Stark is a great warrior, a loving husband and father, a decent administrator, but a terrible politician. His strength and honor proves inadequate at dealing with the sly, conniving players of King's Landing. He faces antagonism from Queen Cersei Lannister and her rich, powerful House Lannister of Casterly Rock.

While investigating the death of Jon Arryn, the previous Hand of the King, Ned discovers a dangerous truth: that all of Robert's children are actually the product of the incestuous relationship between Cersei Lannister and her twin brother Jaime Lannister.

Before telling the truth to Robert, Ned warns Cersei, asking her to flee with her children, because he knows Robert would never let her or her children stay alive. But Ned's concern for her children's lives proves to be his undoing. Shortly after Ned's warning, Robert conveniently dies during hunting. Her petulant teenage son Joffrey "Baratheon" becomes the new king. When Ned protests against it, questioning Joffrey's legitimacy, Cersei has him arrested.

Ned is declared a traitor, with Cersei planning to send into permanent exile to the far North, but at the last moment Joffrey demands Ned's execution. In a heartbreaking scene, Ned Stark, the protagonist of the first season, the good, noble hero, gets beheaded in front of his two young daughters.

In the game of thrones, you win, or you die, and Ned Stark never got close to winning.

2. Robert Baratheon

In the beginning of the show, Robert Baratheon, played by Mark Addy, is the King of Westeros, Lord of the Seven Kingdoms, Protector of the Realm. He's Ned's best friend, and the duo have a long history together. During the reign of Mad King Aerys, Robert loved Lyanna Stark, Ned's sister, and was supposed to marry her. But Lyanna was abducted by Prince Rhaegar Targaryen. Both Ned's father, Rickard Stark, and brother, Brandon Stark, were killed by the Mad King when they went to King's Landing to protest.

Robert launched a rebellion against the King, and was supported by many noble houses. Eventually, he won the war, and became the new king, toppling the three hundred year old Targaryen dynasty. Robert was a fierce warrior, a war-hammer being his chief weapon. How badass is that?

But Robert's skills as a king were nowhere near as impressive as his battle prowess. He found the administrative work tedious and missed the adrenaline rush of battle. He spent most of his days frequenting brothels and consuming copious amounts of wine. When Lyanna Stark was found dead, Robert was married to Cersei Lannister, a shrewd political maneuver by House Lannister to align them with the now powerful House Baratheon. Robert was deeply damaged by Lyanna's death, and could never bring himself to love Cersei.

In the first season, which takes place fifteen years after Robert's rebellion, we get a taste of the bitter, loveless marriage of Robert and Cersei. The tension between Ned and Cersei creates tension between Robert and Ned, but their friendship remains intact.

Robert dies under suspicious circumstances, killed by a boar while hunting, just as Ned discovers the truth about his children. Before dying, he makes Ned the Protector of the Realm, a title which makes him de facto king until Robert's (supposed) son, Joffrey, reaches suitable age. Of course, that doesn't turn out well.

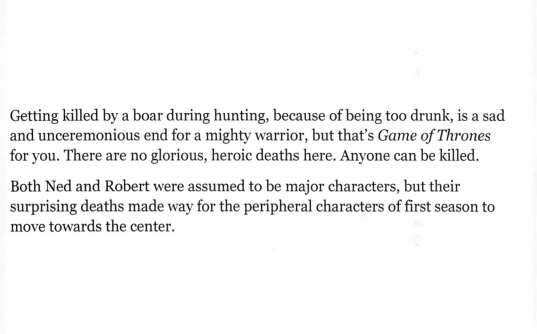

Getting killed by a boar during hunting, because of being too drunk, is a sad and unceremonious end for a mighty warrior, but that's *Game of Thrones* for you. There are no glorious, heroic deaths here. Anyone can be killed.

Both Ned and Robert were assumed to be major characters, but their surprising deaths made way for the peripheral characters of first season to move towards the center.

3. Cersei Lannister

In the first season, Cersei, played by Lena Headey, is the wife of Robert Baratheon, and Queen of the seven kingdoms of Westeros. In the first episode itself we find out that she has an incestuous relationship with her twin brother, Jaime Lannister. *Game of Thrones* is certainly not for the prudish, or the faint-hearted.

Cersei is cynical, spiteful, and quite cunning, politically outwitting Ned Stark, who was planning to tell on her to Robert. It's never made explicit, but heavily implied, that she is responsible for the death of Robert, which couldn't have been more convenient.

Cersei spends most of the show on King's Landing, the place where guile and scheming take precedence over magic and swords. She doesn't show affection or care for anyone except her children and Jaime. After Robert's death she installs her son Joffrey as the King, while she becomes the Queen Regent. She takes many belligerent, short-sighted decisions, like rejecting Ned's son's peace terms, and refusing aid to the Night's Watch.

She has a deeply hateful relationship with Tyrion, her dwarf brother. She blames him for the death of their mother, who died giving birth to Tyrion, and resents him for being a "monster". When Joffrey is mysteriously killed at his wedding in the fourth season, she accuses Tyrion for murder and tries her best to have him killed.

Another woman who gets on Cersei's nerves is Margery Tyrell, the woman who was supposed to be Joffrey's wife and Queen. Margery herself is a political player and manipulates people around her to gain what she wants, which Cersei sees through clearly.

There's also a lot of friction between her and House Lannister patriarch Tywin Lannister. She always tries to assert herself and get what she wants, but is undermined by Tywin, another cunning, manipulative personality. Tywin demands her to marry Loras Tyrell, of House Tyrell, but she refuses, as she doesn't want to get away from Jaime. This proves to be a point of contention between the two.

In the fourth season finale, Tywin dies, and Cersei effectively becomes the most powerful person in Westeros. It'll be fascinating to see where she goes in Season 5, and what she does with her enormous power.

4. Tyrion Lannister

Tyrion Lannister, played by the awesome Peter Dinklage, is one of the show's most popular characters. Tyrion is not just a major character, but the closest the show has to a hero, which is unprecedented in an industry where dwarves are rarely taken seriously.

Tyrion is the son of Tywin Lannister of Casterly Rock, and the brother of Jaime and Cersei Lannister. In the first season, we meet him as a wise-cracking, roguish, lovable imp. He's a modern man in a medieval world, who likes wine and sex over the barbarism of war. We soon find out that his sarcastic exterior is a defense mechanism for his insecurities.

Tyrion's mother died giving birth to him, something for which he has been resented by his family members since his childhood. In the social structure of Westeros, there's no place for "freaks" like Tyrion. The only reason he has managed to survive through his adulthood is because of his noble birth and wealth.

His father, Tywin Lannister, deeply resents him and considers him a shame to his family. Tyrion is aware of his father's antipathy, which pains him, and he expresses his pain through his caustic behavior towards his father. If you read between the lines, it's evident that Tyrion wants his father to be proud of him, and accept him.

Tyrion has a similarly antagonistic relationship with his sister, who openly despises Tyrion. The only person in his family who seems to care about him is his brother Jaime. When Catelyn Stark, Ned's wife, accuses Tyrion of attempting to murder her son and captures him, Jamie openly gets into a sword fight with Ned in the streets of King's Landing. Catelyn takes Tyrion to Vale, where her sister resides, to bring him to justice. Tyrion demands a trial by combat, and a mercenary named Bronn steps up to fight on his behalf. Bronn wins the fight and Tyrion is released.

He's made the Hand of the King by Tywin and in the second season, we see Tyrion outwitting the slimy schemers of King's Landing. His relationships with Cersei and her son King Joffrey get worse through the course of the show.

Towards the end of the second season, Stannis Baratheon, brother of Robert Baratheon, attacks King's Landing, claiming to be the rightful heir to the throne. Tyrion plays a huge part in defending the city, but his contributions are ignored as Tywin, who swoops in at the last minute of the battle, is given all the credit for the victory.

In Season 3, Tyrion is married to Sansa Stark, one of Ned's daughters. This doesn't please Shae, Tyrion's secret lover, who's also Sansa's handmaiden. Tyrion's relationship with Shae progressively deteriorates.

Early on in Season 4, Joffrey is poisoned at his wedding, and Cersei immediately accuses Tyrion of murder. At his trial, people who he had pissed off before come out against him. Tywin intends to send him to the Night's Watch, but Tyrion demands a trial by combat.

Tyrion seeks Bronn's help, but finds out he has been bribed by Cersei. Eventually Oberyn Martell of Dorne, a legendary warrior who had come to King's Landing for Joffrey's wedding, comes forward to volunteer for Tyrion. Oberyn brutally loses the battle, and Tyrion is sentenced to death by his own father.

Tyrion is rescued by Jaime, who arranges to have him shipped to the continent of Essos. But before escaping, Tyrion takes a detour into his father's chambers and finds Shae in his bed. He strangles Shae to death and takes a crossbow to the toilets, looking for his father. He confronts Tywin and kills him, and finally escapes in a ship, hidden in a crate.

Tyrion is now completely broken, emotionally. In Season 5 we'll see him outside Westeros for the first time. It'll be exciting to see what he's up to in a foreign land, and if he'll ever get revenge from his wretched sister.

5. Arya Stark

Arya Stark, played by Maisie Williams, is another one of the show's popular characters. She is Ned Stark's pre-adolescent daughter, who goes with him to King's Landing and watches him die. Unlike her sister, Arya manages to escape and get into thrilling adventures.

 It's hard to find another character in fiction who is simultaneously this badass, tragic, and cute. Arya is a feisty tomboy who prefers playing with swords over dolls. She never backs off and doesn't shy away from getting into a fight, irrespective of the opponent.

In season 1 she gets sword training in King's Landing from an exotic sword-master, Syrio Forel. But that goes south quickly, and Syrio is presumably killed off screen.

After Ned's death, she escapes from the clutches of the Lannisters and disguises herself as a boy. Along the way she makes several scruffy new friends. Arya develops a morbid new habit: reciting the names of all the people she plans to kill, every night. One of the people from her list is Sandor Clegane, aka The Hound, who had killed a friend of hers in Season 1 upon the king's orders.

She's taken captive to Harrenhal, a gloomy castle in the Riverlands. There, she makes an unlikely friend: the mysterious assassin Jaqen H'ghar. With his help, she and her friends escape from Harrenhal. H'ghar offers her to come with him to the Free City of Braavos, but she declines. He gives her a special coin, telling her that she can reach him by showing it to anyone from Braavos and reciting the words "Valar Morghulis".

In Season 3, Arya meets the Brotherhood Without Banners, a guerrilla rebel group working against the Lannisters in the Riverlands. She's first fascinated by the group, but soon becomes disillusioned and tries to escape. She's captured by the Hound, who isn't working for the king anymore. He plans to take her to her mother, Catelyn, and demand bounty.

But just as Arya and The Hound reach their destination, The Twins, they find out that the Stark bannermen are being massacred. Worried, when Arya tries to enter the castle, The Hound knocks her out.

In Season 4, The Hound decides to take her to her aunt Lysa, in Vale. But when they reach there they find out that her Aunt has recently expired. The absurdity of their bad luck makes Arya laugh.

In the fourth season finale, the Hound is gravely injured after a brutal fight, and Arya leaves him to die on his own, ignoring his pleas to be killed. She reaches a ship and meets a man who claims to be from Braavos, and shows her H'ghar's coin. In her final scene, we see her standing at the edge of the ship, looking forward, as it's sailing away from Westeros.

Will Arya meet H'ghar in Season 5 and become a badass assassin? That would be the coolest thing ever.

6. Daenerys Targaryen

Daenerys Targaryen, played by Emilia Clarke, is also one of the show's "good guys". She's a young, idealistic, charismatic leader, and the mother of three dragons. Her story takes place completely outside Westeros, in the continent of Essos. She's the daughter of Aerys "Mad King" Targaryen, and one of the last surviving Targaryens.

She, and her brother Viserys, managed to escape from King's Landing during Robert's Rebellion. In the first season, her brother forces her to marry Khal Drogo, the leader of the Dothrakis, a tribal group inspired by the Mongols. Viserys marries his sister to Drogo upon one condition: that Drogo will invade Westeros and install the Targaryen siblings as rulers, heralding a revival of the Targaryen dynasty.

Daenerys adapts to the Dothraki culture, starts loving her husband, and learns his language. She also becomes pregnant with his son, who the Dothrakis believe to be a long-prophesied conqueror, the "Stallion Who Mounts the World". Daenerys meets an ex-Knight from Westeros, Jorah Mormont, who gifts her three old dragon eggs, which are assumed to have turned into stone over time.

Viserys grows impatient, and his petulance and disrespect towards his sister and the Dothrakis angers Drogo, who kills him by pouring molten gold over his head.

Drogo gets an infection from a minor wound, which makes him gravely ill. Daenerys asks for the help of a witch, who saves Drogo's life, but sends him into a vegetative state. The witch's magic on Drogo also causes Daenerys' child to be stillborn. Daenerys mercy-kills Drogo, and becomes the new leader of the Dothrakis. Jorah Mormont becomes her chief advisor.

At the end of season 1, she burns the witch and hatches the dragon eggs. Three little dragons pop out of the eggs and treat her as their mother. She is revealed to be invulnerable to fire. In season 2, she visits the city of Qarth, where her dragons are stolen by a warlock. She eventually recovers them, and the warlock is burnt by dragon fire.

By Season 3, her dragons have grown to the size of big dogs, which makes them excellent bodyguards, but not big enough to lead a war into Westeros. Daenerys realizes the dragons alone won't win her a war, and that she needs soldiers. She trades the Unsullied, an army of 8000 castrated slave-soldiers, for one of her dragons. But the dragon kills the buyer, and Daenerys proceeds to free the slaves of the city, commanding them to kill their masters.

Daenerys invades and frees slaves from several other cities, eventually settling in Meeren, where she stays till the end of season four. As the Queen of Meeren, she finds out that upsetting the status quo comes at a cost, and radical change is turbulent, when the former masters and former slaves of the city bring up their problems to her. Her dragons have become considerably big now, and are preying on farmers and herders. In the fourth season finale, she finds out that one of her dragons, Drogon, has killed a three year-old child. She is unable to find Drogon, but locks up the other two of her dragons in chains, while crying.

7. Jorah Mormont

Jorah Mormont, played by Iain Glen, is a Westerosi Knight in exile, who was sentenced to death for slave trade, which is illegal in Westeros. In Season 1, he acts as an informant for Varys, King's Landing's spymaster, and spies on Viserys and his sister. He's the one who gives the dragon eggs to Daenerys. As the two grow closer, he develops feelings for her, and abandons his spying duties. He saves her from an assassination attempt, earning her trust.

It's made clear that Jorah loves Daenerys, but she never reciprocates his feelings. His relationship with her is the only that survives from the pilot till the fourth season. Towards the last third of Season 4, Daenerys finds out that he used to spy on her, and banishes him from Meeren, severing all her ties with him.

8. Jon Snow

Jon Snow, played by Kit Harrington, is the illegitimate son of Ned Stark. In Westeros, illegitimate children are derogatorily referred to as "bastards". Bastards can't inherit anything from their fathers, not even their House names. The surnames of bastards are determined by their location in Westeros. Each kingdom has a separate bastard surname, based on the geography. Every bastard in the North is a Snow. Similarly, a bastard in the arid Dorne region has the surname Sand.

Jon has grown up with the other Stark children, but he has never been accepted by Catelyn Stark, Ned's wife. For her, Jon is a walking reminder of Ned's infidelity. Jon has a loving relationship with Arya, whom he gifts a sword in the first season, which Arya names 'Needle'.

In the early episodes of the show, Jon parts from his family and joins the Night's Watch. The Night's Watch is a brotherhood of men, with thousands of years of history, sworn to patrol The Wall, a gigantic ancient structure made of ice, and protect the kingdom from everything that lies beyond the Wall. In the first scene of the show itself, we get a glimpse of what lies beyond – zombies; Ice zombies, to be more specific. In the second season finale, we get a proper look at the feared supernatural race called the White Walkers. As winter is approaching Westeros, the White Walkers are marching towards the Wall, and presumably planning to take over Westeros and end civilization.

It isn't just ice zombies that exist north of the wall. There are several disenfranchised human tribes, called Wildlings that live in clusters and have an antagonistic relationship with the Night's Watch, as the Wildings often breach the wall and raid villages in the North. During the beginning of the show, White Walkers are believed to be a myth, and it's mostly Wildlings that the Night's Watch are expected to deal with.

Initially, Jon has a hard time at the Wall, but he eventually manages to make friends. One of his closest friends is Samwell Tarly, a pudgy, meek young man who'd rather read books than patrol the Wall.

Because of the approaching winter and the threat of the White Walkers, all the Wildling tribes are united into an army by an ex-Night's Watch brother, Mance Rayder, who formulates a plan to attack and breach the Wall.

In Season 3, Jon Snow infiltrates the Wildling army and earns the trust of Mance Rayder. He falls in love with a feisty Wildling woman, Ygritte. Ultimately, Jon abandons the Wildlings and returns to the Wall to warn his compatriots about their plans, thus breaking Ygritte's heart. In Season 4, when a group of Wildlings attack the Wall, the rag-tag Night's Watch brothers, badly outnumbered, fight bravely under Jon's leadership and manage to defend the Wall that night. Ygritte is killed by an arbitrary arrow, and spends her last moments in Jon's arms, with him filled with tears.

The next day, Stannis Baratheon, brother of Robert Baratheon, reaches the Wall and comprehensively defeats the Wildling army.

9. Stannis Baratheon

Stannis, played by Stephen Dillane, is the younger brother of Robert Baratheon. He's an uptight, humorless, and stubborn leader, preoccupied with delivering proper justice. He's also a competent naval and military commander. His absolute sense of right and wrong can sometimes seem harsh, like when he chopped off the fingers of Davos Seaworth, who saved him and his army during a siege by bringing in food, because of his past crimes as a smuggler. Davos has been a trusted advisor to Stannis since.

His stubborn sense of fairness doesn't win him many friends. During Robert's Rebellion, he fought alongside him against the Targaryens, but wasn't appreciated for his efforts by Robert. When Ned finds out the truth about Cersei and her kids, he informs Stannis about it. Instead of taking the throne for himself, which he could have, Ned backs Stannis as the rightful King, but because of Stannis' unpopularity, Ned isn't supported by many people.

Stannis lives in Dragonstone, a brooding fortress that used to be a Targaryen stronghold. After Robert's death, Stannis claims to be the rightful heir to the throne, but considerable portion of the Baratheon army pledges allegiance to Renly Baratheon, the youngest Baratheon brother, who's more charismatic and popular than Stannis.

Stannis follows a new religion of the God R'hllor, foreign to Westeros, preached by a sexy, mysterious priestess, Melisandre. There's a lot of tension between Melisandre and Davos Seaworth, who offer differing advices to Stannis, and often Stannis is forced to choose between the two.

Renly is killed by a magic baby ghost demon (we really don't know what it was, except that it was really creepy), and Stannis finally commands the entire Baratheon army. He attacks King's Landing through the sea, and faces the defensive forces of King's Landing at the Battle of Blackwater. His assault is resisted by Tyrion's strategic cunning, and he's ultimately defeated by Tywin Lannister's forces. The army of House Tyrell was aligned with Renly, but after Renly's death, they sided with Tywin. Stannis' forces aren't able to survive the combined armies of House Lannister and House Tyrell.

Stannis returns to Dragonstone after his defeat. The Night's Watch send letters to every powerful Lord, asking for help from the marching Wildling army. While all the other Lords ignore the plea, Stannis is convinced by Davos to defend the Wall. In Season 4, Stannis and Davos travel to Braavos and convince the Iron Bank of Braavos to back them.

In the fourth season finale, Stannis attacks the Wildlings beyond the wall and effortlessly defeats them. The undisciplined Wildling army is no match for the trained, battle-hardened Baratheon army.

With Stannis, Jon, and Melisandre at the Wall, it'll be interesting to see what events transpire in the fifth season.

10. Jaime Lannister

Jaime Lannister, played by Nikolaj Coster-Waldau, is the brother/lover of Cersei Lannister, and the eldest son of Tywin Lannister. Like every Lannister, he's a bit twisted. In the first episode itself, we see him pushing a kid off a window to keep his incest a secret. Ew, right?

Jaime is a legendary swordsman and a member of the Kingsguard, a group of elite Knights meant to serve and protect the King. He has been a knight since the days of Mad King Aerys. Towards the last phase of Robert's Rebellion, when the Targaryens were at the brink of defeat, the Mad King ordered Jaime to kill his father, Tywin, who had switched his allegiance to Robert. The Mad King also had plans to burn the entire city of King's Landing. Jaime betrayed his Kingsguard vows, and killed the Mad King as well as his pyromancer. He was forever maligned by this event, as breaking an oath is considered a taboo in Westeros. After he killed the Mad King, Ned Stark entered the room and instantly judged him for his act. Since that day, Jaime is infamously known as the Kingslayer. That sounds like a cool nickname, but for Jaime it means an eternal blot on his honor.

Jaime sincerely loves his sister, and she's the only woman he has ever been with. The same cannot be said about his sister, though. Jaime is the only person in his family who cares about Tyrion, and watches his back. Tywin wants Jaime to quit the Kingsguard and inherit Casterly Rock, but Jaime has no interest in his family's legacy.

In the first episode of the show, he and Cersei are found in a compromising position by Bran Stark, one of Ned Stark's younger sons. Jaime immediately pushes Bran off the window, which cripples him and inflicts him with selective amnesia about the event. In the first season, Jaime has a sarcastic, smug, self-centered personality. His confidence in his sword-fighting skills makes him extremely cocky.

When Tyrion is taken hostage by Catelyn, Jaime confronts Ned in the streets and fights him. When Robb Stark, Ned's eldest son, launches a war against the Lannisters, Jaime is at the frontlines. Through one of Robb's clever strategic maneuvers, Jaime is kidnapped and brought to the Stark camp. He's eventually freed by Catelyn, in the hopes of getting back her two daughters from King's Landing. She sends Jaime with Brienne of Tarth, a loyal and honorable lady knight.

Jaime initially makes fun of Brienne, and her sincerity, but gradually develops a begrudging respect for her. Both of them are captured by the men of House Bolton, who slice off Jaime's right wrist. With his biggest strength gone, Jaime loses his confidence, and shows a shift in his personality. House Bolton ultimately betrays the Starks and sides with Tywin, and Jaime is released to return to King's Landing. By this time, Jaime and Brienne have formed a close bond, which doesn't escape Cersei's notice.

Jaime's existential crisis followed by his hand amputation makes him rethink about his legacy, his honor. The Jaime of fourth season is far less cynical and cocky. When Tyrion is sentenced to death, he helps him escape King's Landing.

11. Tywin Lannister

Tywin Lannister, played by Charles Dance, is one of the most cunning, ruthless characters in *Game of Thrones*. He has a steely, intimidating personality, and is tough with his children, whom he doesn't show any outward affection of love. The thing that matters the most to him is his family's legacy. Tywin doesn't mince words, and always knows how to get what he wants. His diligence and intelligence has made him the richest man of Westeros, and House Lannister one of the most powerful noble houses.

Tywin's father was a weak man; under whose rule House Lannister was in a state of decline. When one of the vassal houses sworn to them, House Reyne of Castamere, rebelled against them, Tywin led the charge to suppress the rebellion and thoroughly defeated the Reynes. He torched Castamere, and executed every member of House Reyne. This established his fearful reputation all over Westeros. A folk song was made based on this event, called "The Rains of Castamere". It's effectively the theme song of the Lannisters.

Tywin was the Hand of the King under the Mad King, and was tentatively on his side when Robert started his rebellion. But when he realized Robert was winning the war, he immediately changed sides and betrayed the king.

In Season 2, during the Battle of Blackwater, Tywin saves King's Landing by showing up at the last minute, along with the army of House Tyrell, and defeats Stannis. He becomes the new Hand of the King, replacing Tyrion.

In Season 3, he secretly makes a deal with House Frey and House Bolton, who betray the Starks and kill Robb Stark, his mother and all their bannermen at a wedding, which is infamously knows as the Red Wedding. The massacre of the Red Wedding puts an end to the War of the Five Kings, bringing political stability to the realm.

Tywin has a difficult relationship with all his children, especially Tyrion. He considers Tyrion a disappointment, and a disgrace, while Tyrion resents him for never caring anout him. When Tyrion is accused of Joffrey's murder, and loses the trial by combat, Tywin sentences him to death. After

Tyrion is rescued by Jaime, he goes up to Tywin's chamber pots (toilet) and shoots him with a crossbow.

With Tywin dead, Cersei now becomes the most powerful person in Westeros.

12. Catelyn Stark

Catelyn, played by Michelle Fairley, is Ned's wife, and the mother of Arya Stark. She was supposed to marry Brandon Stark, Ned's older brother, until he was killed by the Mad King. Catelyn's maiden surname is Tully, and she's originally from the Riverlands. Her culture is very different from that of the North, but she tries her best to adapt to its customs. She is an extremely devoted wife and mother, who'll go to any lengths to protect her children.

After the death of Jon Arryn, her sister, Lysa Arryn, writes to her implicating the Lannisters. This makes her highly distrustful towards them. After Bran, her son, is crippled, there's an assassination attempt on him by an unknown assailant. By this time, Ned is already at King's Landing with Robert. Catelyn immediately travels to King's Landing to warn Ned about the Lannisters. In King's Landing, her childhood friend and the Master of Coin, Petyr Baelish, identifies the weapon used in the assassination attempt as Tyrion's.

On her way over returning from King's Landing, Catelyn encounters Tyrion and takes him hostage. She takes him to Vale, to her sister, but Tyrion escapes through trial by combat.

After Ned's death, she helps her son Robb in his war with the Lannisters. She releases Jaime from their camp, after he is painstakingly captured by Robb, hoping that he will return the Stark girls from King's Landing.

At the end of Season 3, Catelyn, Robb, and their entire army is killed in the Red Wedding, when House Bolton and House Frey betray them after colluding with Tywin.

13. Sansa Stark

Sansa, played by Sophie Turner, is the eldest daughter of Catelyn and Ned. Early on in the show, she has a crush on Prince Joffrey, Cersei's son, to whom she's betrothed. Her interests are very different from Arya's, and the two constantly bicker and fight over their differences. After Ned is taken prisoner, she and Arya are effectively hostages in King's Landing. She soon finds out that Joffrey is a sadistic bully, as he tortures and humiliates her at every turn.

She convinces her father to plead guilty and be sent to the Wall, but at the last moment Joffrey orders for Ned's execution. Sansa watches her father get beheaded in front of her. Joffrey retracts his betrothal and instead decides to marry Margaery Tyrell, from House Tyrell of the Reach. Sansa is forcibly married to Tyrion, who is one of the few people who tries to be nice to Sansa.

After Robb's death, Sansa is believed to be the only Stark alive. Her younger siblings – Arya, Bran and Rickon– are all assumed to be dead.

As soon as Joffrey dies at his wedding, Sansa is rescued by through Petyr Baelish, who takes her to Vale, to her aunt, Lysa Arryn. She discovers that Petyr has romantic feelings towards her. She presents herself in Vale as Alayne, Petyr's niece. No one except Lysa knows her true identity.

Lysa madly loves Petyr and marries him, but when she finds out Petyr has interest in Sansa, she threatens her. Petyr coaxes Lysa and finally pushes her through the moon door – a trap door at a great height, below which there's nothing until the ground.

Sansa is now with Petyr at Vale, and learning to grow out of her naiveté and pick up the skills of manipulation. Her arc is very different from her sister Arya; it's more subtle and emotionally brutal. Let's hope in the upcoming seasons she gets some peace.

14. Joffrey Baratheon

It's unlikely there will ever be a character on television as hated as Joffrey. Played by Jack Gleeson, who you might remember as That Kid from Batman Begins, Joffrey has a legion of haters from around the world, who, throughout the last four years, have only wished one thing: his death.

Joffrey is what you'll get when you give a high school bully the powers of a monarch. He's a sadistic, cowardly, entitled little psychopathic brat who gets off on humiliating and torturing others. There's nothing respectable about him, he can't hold his own in a fight against anyone, he hides behind his mother every time he gets scared, and yet, he lords over others and torments them at every chance he gets.

In the beginning of the show he's introduced as Robert's son, but soon we find out that he's the product of incest between Jaime and Cersei.

One of the people most harassed by Joffrey is Sansa. In Winterfell, when they meet, his obnoxiousness seems relatively normal, but once they go to King's Landing, his petulance reaches epic proportions. After Robert's death, Cersei installs Joffrey as the new ruler, which Ned protests. Ned is accused of being a traitor, and imprisoned. Cersei plans to send Ned to the Wall, but at the last minute, Joffrey orders for his execution. Things get worse for Sansa. He beats her, drags her to his throne room, and strips her. His whimsical evil frightens and disgusts everyone around him, including the people of King's Landing, among whom he isn't very popular.

Joffrey rejects Sansa and gets betrothed to Margaery Tyrell. He has a considerably better relationship with her, as she's able to manipulate her way around him.

The one person who is able to get some retribution over Joffrey is Tyrion. He slaps him several times through the series, and isn't afraid to speak what he truly thinks of him. Joffrey looks for new opportunities every day to harass Tyrion.

Joffrey is poisoned at his own wedding, and Cersei instantly accuses Tyrion for his murder. It's hinted later that Olenna Tyrell, Margaery's grandmother and House Tyrell matriarch, colluded with Petyr Baelish to have him killed.

15. Bran Stark

Brandon Stark, played by Isaac Hempstead-Wright, is Ned's second youngest son, the youngest being Rickon Stark. Ned has named him after his deceased older brother. In the first episode, he's pushed off a window by Jaime Lannister, after he witnesses Jaime and Cersei having sex. Bran is paralyzed, and is unable to remember who pushed him, or what happened before the fall. An assassin attempts to kill him, but he's saved by his direwolf, Summer. Bran often has dreams about following a three eyed raven. Because of his paralysis, he's carried everywhere by Hodor, a mentally challenged simpleton.

With both Catelyn and Ned absent from Winterfell, it's attacked and seized by Theon Greyjoy, from House Greyjoy of Iron Islands. Bran and Rickon escape with the help of Osha, a Wildling, and Hodor.

In Season 3 they meet Jojen Reed, and his sister Meera, who claim to be their benefactors. Jojen has the special ability to see the past and the future. He makes Bran aware of his superpower: the ability to control the bodies of animals. In the world of *Game of Thrones* it's called warging. Jojen also claims to be aware of the three-eyed raven and promises to take Bran to him.

Osha is distrustful of the siblings, and gets into an argument with them when Jojen insists they must go beyond the Wall. Bran orders Osha to take Rickon and go the holdfast of Greatjon Umber, one of House Stark's loyal bannermen. Osha and Rickon separate from the group. Bran goes beyond the wall along with Hodor and the siblings.

In Season 4, as the group is close to their destination, they're attacked by zombies, and Jojen Reed is killed. Bran wargs into Hodor and fights the zombies. A mysterious child throws firebombs at the zombies and asks Bran and the others to get inside his cave. Inside the cave, Bran finally meets the three-eyed raven, who turns out to be an old man with his body fused to a tree. Bran asks him if he'll be able to walk again. The raven replies: "You will never walk in your life, but you will fly."

16. Robb Stark

Robb Stark, played by Richard Madden, is Ned Stark's eldest son. Like his father, he's honorable and loyal. He's also a great tactician and skillful commander.

After Ned's death, Robb unites various houses of the North under his banner and leads the charge in his war against the Lannisters. The fight between the Starks and the Lannisters eventually becomes the War of the Five Kings, as other parties stake their claim to the throne after Robert's death.

Robb doesn't want the throne; instead he fights for the North's secession from the crown. In the first season, he captures Jaime Lannister, and hopes to use him for leverage, but Catelyn release him in exchange for his promise to return her girls.

Robb wins battle after battle over the Lannisters, but politically, his situation gets worse. He trusts Theon Greyjoy, with whom he has a brotherly relation, to negotiate with his own father at the Iron Islands, but Theon betrays Robb's trust and seizes Winterfell. Bran and Rickon escape, but everyone believes them to be dead, and Winterfell is burned.

Robb falls in love with Talisa Maegyr and marries her, breaking his oath to Walder Frey, one of his allies, to marry one of his daughters. When Richard Karstark, one of his bannermen, kills two Lannister prisoners who're children, Robb executes him and loses the support of the Karstarks.

To improve his political standing, Robb decides to negotiate with Walder Frey. Frey agrees to put aside Robb's transgression and provide support to the Starks, if Catelyn's brother Edmure marries one of his daughters. The Starks agree with the deal, and wedding arrangements are made.

At the wedding, Talisa tells Robb she's pregnant. After the bride and the groom exit the wedding hall, the Freys close the door and musicians at the top berth start playing The Rains of Castamere. Catelyn realizes something is wrong and finds out that Roose Bolton, one of their bannermen, is wearing chainmail. She realizes that the Boltons and the Freys have betrayed them and tries to warn Robb. The musicians bring out crossbows and start shooting at the Starks. Talisa is brutally stabbed in her womb. Robb is killed by Roose. Walder Frey sits in his chair and enjoys the massacre.

Outside the hall, all men associated with the Starks are killed by the Freys and the Boltons. The Stark forces are decimated, and the War of the Five Kings is over.

17. Theon Greyjoy

Theon Greyjoy, played by Alfie Allen, is probably the most unfortunate character in *Game of Thrones*, and that's saying something. He was born to Lord Balon Greyjoy of the Iron Islands. The Iron Islanders are basically the Vikings of Westeros. They have strong naval fleets and believe in looting and pillaging to get their food, instead of, you know, agriculture. It's considered shameful for an Iron Islander to grow his own food.

Eight years before the beginning of the story, Balon Greyjoy launches a rebellion against King Robert. Robert demolishes them in the war and Balon surrenders. Ned takes Theon as hostage, so that Balon thinks twice before trying any mischief again.

Ned raises Theon as his own son. He lives with the Stark kids as their sibling, and is especially close to Robb.

Against his mother's advice, Robb sends Theon the Iron Islands to negotiate with Balon, during his war against the Iron Throne. Theon betrays Robb's trust and seizes Winterfell. He calls himself the Prince of Winterfell and burns two farm children, claiming them to be Bran and Rickon.

Theon is knocked out by his fellow Iron Islanders, who don't take him seriously. He's captured by Ramsay Snow, the bastard of Roose Bolton. Ramsay tortures and interrogates Theon and finds out that Bran and Rickon are still alive.

Ramsay puts Theon through elaborate psychological and physical torture, completely destroying Theon's psyche. He castrates him, and renames him as 'Reek', which Theon eventually accepts as his new name.

In Season 4, Theon is treated as a house pet by Ramsay, who makes him do menial tasks for him. Theon's sister, Yara, attempts to rescue him, but Theon believes her to be an illusion and refuses to leave.

Theon/Reek is currently at a very miserable place, let's hope that he gets some redemption by the time the show ends.

18. Sandor Clegane, aka The Hound

Sandor Clegane, played by Rory McCann, is mostly known by his nickname: The Hound, because of his savagery and faithfulness towards his masters. He's a fierce warrior with a nihilistic worldview, though he's not completely without mercy. When he was a kid, his older brother, Gregor Clegane aka the Mountain, put his face into the fire, permanently scarring half of his face. Since then, Sandor has a phobia of fire.

In the first season he's introduced as Joffrey's bodyguard, who begrudgingly obeys every one of his capricious and petulant master's commands. When Joffrey becomes King, the Hound joins the Kingsguard. During the Battle of Blackwater, an explosion and ensuing use of fire in the battle freaks him out, and he abruptly abandons the Kingsguard, and leaves King's Landing.

In Season 3, he's captured by the Brotherhood Without Banners, who subject him to trial by combat. Sandor fights against a man using a flaming sword, but manages to win. He's allowed to leave, but he hides in the vicinity. When Arya escapes the brotherhood, he kidnaps her and plans to take her to her mother in The Twins, where Catelyn's brother is supposed to marry one of Walder Frey's daughters.

But as soon as he arrives there with Arya, he finds out there's something wrong, and knocks Arya out when she tries to go into the castle.

He then decides to take her to her aunt Lysa in Vale, but when they reach there, they find out that Lysa has just died. While returning, the Hound has a brutal altercation with Brienne, which fatally wounds him. Arya leaves him to die as he begs her to kill him.

19. Petyr Baelish

Petyr, played by Aidan Gillen, is more commonly known as Littlefinger. He's a shrewd, manipulative figure who never makes his intentions clear. He grew up with Catelyn, who was his unrequited childhood love. At the start of the show, he's the Master of Coin (one of the positions at the king's small council), and the owner of many brothels.

He betrays Ned and sides with Cersei, after leading Ned to believe he would do otherwise. In Season 4, he rescues Sansa from King's Landing, and reveals himself to be behind Joffrey's death. He's attracted towards Sansa, who reminds him of Catelyn. He marries Lysa Arryn, who is then killed by him, after she threatens Sansa. It is also revealed that Lysa had killed her husband Jon Arryn upon Littlefinger's instructions. Jon Arryn's death was the catalyst to the events of *Game of Thrones*, so this revelation means Littlefinger was the mastermind behind everything that has happened in the show. Upon hindsight, it becomes clear that he manipulated the Lannisters and the Starks to the brink of war.

20. Varys

Varys, aka The Spider, is played by Conleth Hill. He has a vast network of spies spanning across continents through which he gains information for the king. He holds a position in the king's small council, called Master of Whisperers. He's a eunuch, castrated at a young age by a sorcerer. He ultimately captures the sorcerer, and in one of the episodes, we see him holding him prisoner in a box.

Varys considers Littlefinger his chief opponent, whose lies and deceit he sees through easily. When Ned is imprisoned, he visits him in his cell and expresses his sympathy. Varys is one of the few people in King's Landing with whom Tyrion's relation isn't utterly bad. They aren't outright friends, but Tyrion trusts him more than any of the other small council members.

In the fourth season finale, Varys helps Jaime in rescuing Tyrion. When he realizes that Tyrion has killed Tywin, he gets on the boat with him, and sits alongside the box in which Tyrion is hiding.

21. Brienne

Brienne of Tarth, played by Gwendoline Christie, is an honorable Knight, who becomes part of Renly's Kingsguard shortly before his assassination. She pledges her allegiance to Catelyn who orders her to take Jaime to King's Landing, and bring back her daughters. During her journey with Jaime, she develops feelings for him as the two share several dangerous adventures. In the third season, the Bolton men make her fight a bear. She's saved by Jaime.

At King's Landing, she faces a jealous and vicious Cersei. Jaime sends her to find the Stark girls, along with Podrick, who used to be Tyrion's squire. Along their away she meets Arya and the Hound. She identifies Arya and asks her to come with her. The Hound sees Lannister gold on Brienne, which makes him suspicious of her. The Hound and Brienne get into a ruthless fight, which leaves the Hound gravely injured. Arya escapes and Brienne continues searching for her.

22. Margaery Tyrell

Margaery Tyrell, played by Natalie Dormer, is an ambitious young woman from House Tyrell. She's initially betrothed to Renly, but after his death the Tyrells shift their support to the Lannisters. Margaery offers herself to Joffrey, who agrees to marry her and rejects Sansa.

At their wedding, Joffrey is poisoned, and Margaery's ambitions of becoming the Queen are again put on hold. Undeterred by the event, she plans to marry Tommen Baratheon, Joffrey's younger brother and successor.

Margaery has a difficult relationship with Cersei, who sees through her manipulation and resents her for her youth and beauty.

The biggest influence on Margaery is her grandmother, Olenna Tyrell, who's hinted as the one responsible for Joffrey's death.

23. Samwell Tarly

Samwell Tarly, played by John Bradley-West, is a pudgy, cowardly member of the Night's Watch who's better at reading books than using a sword. He strikes a friendship with Jon Snow, who watches his back against bullies.

Sam falls in love with Gilly, a Wildling girl who was sexually abused by her father, and tries to take care of her and her daughter. In the third season, Gilly and her kid are attacked by a White Walker. Sam confronts the creature and manages to kill it accidentally. Sam is the only known person to have killed a White Walker. In the ninth episode of the fourth season, Sam overcomes his cowardice and faces the Wildling army courageously. He survives the battle, but loses many of his friends.

24. Melisandre

Melisandre, played by Dutch actress Carice van Houten, is a priestess of a new religion that's creeping into Westeros – the religion of the Lord of Light. She claims to have magical powers, and helps Stannis in his quest for the Iron Throne.

Melisandre is a religious fanatic who doesn't take heretics lightly. She becomes the closest advisor of Stannis Baratheon, and her words often collide with the views of Davos Seaworth, who has been with Stannis for over a decade.

Stannis' wife is a big devotee of the religion and places unquestioning faith on Melisandre and her words.

In Season 2, she has sex with Stannis, and gives birth to a ghost demon that kills Renly. Stannis himself doesn't believe a great deal in her religion, but keeps her around because of her magical abilities.

In Season 3, she burns three leeches in the name of three kings – Robb Stark, Joffrey Baratheon, and Balon Greyjoy – claiming the ritual would lead to their deaths. Soon after that, Robb Stark dies at the Red Wedding, and Joffrey dies at his own wedding. Balon Greyjoy better watch out.

In the Season 4 finale, when Stannis and his forces are at the Wall, Melisandre gives a creepy look at Jon Snow, indicating interest in him.

25. Davos Seaworth

Davos Seaworth, played by Liam Cunningham, is a landed knight who used to be a smuggler, until he saved Stannis and his forces in a siege, during Robert's War, by smuggling food into his castle. He became a knight, but also had his fingers chopped off by Stannis for being a smuggler.

We meet him in the second season, when he's trying to get himself heard over Melisandre to Stannis. He often gives counsel that goes against Melisandre's advice. He tells Stannis to make peace with Renly, and fight with Joffrey together, but Stannis goes with Melisandre, who produces a ghost demon that kills Renly.

Davos has a paternal relationship with Stannis' daughter, Shireen. Davos is illiterate, so Shireen teaches him how to read by the help of her children's books. Davos manages to read a letter from the Wall asking for help. Davos convinces Stannnis to go to the wall, saying a true king protects his kingdom irrespective of the cost.

When Stannis and Davos go to Braavos to get the financial backing of the Iron Bank, it's Davos who convinces the bankers to support Stannis, claiming him to be a just and fair man.

26. Ramsay Snow

Ramsay Snow, played by Iwan Rheon, is the greatest sadistic psychopath in *Game of Thrones*. He's the bastard of Roose Bolton, who betrayed the Starks at the Red Wedding.

We first meet Ramsay as he's torturing Theon, putting him through elaborate physical and psychological abuses. He manages to get Theon to reveal that Bran and Rickon are alive. He names him 'Reek', and obliterates his sense of self. By Season 4, Theon acts like his pet dog, obeying his every command, calling himself Reek.

With Theon's help, Ramsay is able to take Moat Catlin from Iron Islanders, who are then brutally mutilated and killed. Roose Bolton, impressed with his son, declares him legitimate. Ramsay is no longer a bastard. He's now Ramsay Bolton.

27. Ygritte

Ygritte, played by the gorgeous Rose Leslie, is a Wildling woman who falls in love with Jon Snow. She's a fiery young woman with excellent archery skills, who doesn't let anyone get to her. Her catchphrase is: "You know nothing, Jon Snow!" She uses that line in almost every second scene.

When Jon betrays her and the Wildings, she is heartbroken, and deposits three arrows in Jon, but he survives the wounds.

She attacks the Wall along with other Wildings, and is killed by the arrow of a young kid. She dies in Jon's arms. The next day, Jon cremates her.

28. Bronn

Bronn, played by Jerome Flynn, is an amoral mercenary who volunteers for trial by combat on behalf of Tyrion in Vale, in the first season. He wins the combat and saves Tyrion's life. Tyrion employs him as his bodyguard.

Bronn is highly cynical and pragmatic, and will do anything if you pay him enough money. He likes Tyrion and the two constantly bicker with each other, like old married couples.

During Tyrion's trial for Joffrey's murder, Bronn is paid off by Cersei, and married into high society. He refuses to fight for him in the trial by combat, expressing doubt over his ability to take down the Mountain.

Conclusion

The status quo has been completely dismantled in the fourth season. The War of Five Kings is over. Joffrey is dead. Tywin is dead. Tyrion and Arya are heading outside Westeros. Stannis is at the wall. All the pieces of the board are now scattered, and the game can go anywhere from here.

It's hard to predict what will happen in the fifth season, unless you've read the books, of course. It'll be awesome to see how Cersei reacts when she finds out that not only has Tyrion escaped, but he has also killed her father.

Arya is heading off to Braavos. Will she meet Jaqen H'ghar? I'm sure the fans would love to see her become an assassin, but knowing this show, it's a safe bet that it won't be that simple.

Tyrion and Varys are together now. Their scenes were always a pleasure to watch, so their upcoming adventures should be interesting.

It doesn't look like Daenerys is getting to Westeros any time soon, and firing Jorah might not have been the best choice. With her dragons starting to cause trouble, will her greatest strength become her biggest liability?

Let's hope poor Theon gets some relief, and Ramsay dies in a fire. With Stannis at the Wall, and the Boltons controlling the North, it's likely that they'll face off at one point. What is Melisandre, the preacher of the Lord of Light, going to do at the Wall? Does she have some wicked plans for Jon?

There are a lot more questions that fans have in their minds right now, the most anxious of them being about the release of the next books in the series. The fifth season will come out around April, 2015, going by the premiere dates of previous seasons. The show has already covered three books, and there are two more books left. Will the show catch up to the book series? Will George R.R. Martin be able to come out with the next book in time?

We'll have to wait till a couple of more years to find out. If the show overtakes the books, there's very little chance that HBO will stall it to accommodate Martin. But don't be worried, Martin has already told the show-runners the ending to his series. Is it a happy ending? Well, if you think this has a happy ending, you haven't been paying attention.

Other Books You Might Enjoy:

Game of Thrones: The Ultimate Game of Thrones Character Description Guide (Includes 39 Game of Thrones Characters)

True Blood: A True Blood Series Character Description Quick Guide (Catch Up To Everyone Else In No Time!)

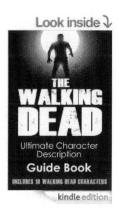

The Walking Dead: Ultimate Character Description Guide Book (Includes 18 Walking Dead Characters)

Game of Thrones 100 Question Trivia Game For True Fans: A Game of Thrones Challenge For Every Occasion (1-4 Game of Thrones Players)

Look inside ↓

THE
**WALKING
DEAD**

THE ULTIMATE WALKING DEAD TRIVIA
GAME TO TEST YOUR KNOWLEDGE

kindle edition

The Walking Dead Trivia Game (80 Questions)

BONUS: Free Books & Special Offers

I want to thank you again for reading this book! I would like to give you access to a great service that will e-mail you notifications when we have FREE books available. You will have FREE access to some great titles before they get marked at the normal retail price that everyone else will pay. This is a no strings attached offer simply for being a great customer.

*Simply go to www.globalizedhealing.com to get free books.

21540825R00032

Printed in Great Britain
by Amazon